Edith Rylander | *They've Packed Up the Rock and Roll*

Edith Rylander

They've Packed Up the Rock and Roll

Poems 1955 – 2018

Red Dragonfly Press

ISBN 978-1-945063-27-5 paper

Library of Congress Control Number: 2019933972

Some of the poems included in this collection have appeared, sometimes in different forms, in the print magazines *Arizona Quarterly*, *Sticks and Stones*, *Milkweed Chronicle*, *W.A.R.M. Journal*, *Sing, Heavenly Muse!*, *Loonfeather*, *North Coast Review*, *North Country Anvil*, *Black Dirt*, *Georgia Review*, *Everywhere*, *ProCreation*, and *Sidewalks*; online in John Caddy's "Morning Earth: Invite to Write"; and in the anthologies *Poets Who Haven't Moved to Minneapolis*, *Essential Love*, *Minnesota Poetry Calendar 1999*, *Minnesota Poetry Calendar 2000*, *Beloved on the Earth*, and *County Lines*.

Dates of poems are dates of composition, not publication. If a poem was under revision for a period of time, the listed dates represent the time from first draft to finished form.

Designed and typeset by Scott King
    using Warnock Pro (text) & Quadraat Sans (titles)

Published by Red Dragonfly Press
    P. O. Box 98
    Northfield, MN 55057
    www.reddragonflypress.org

Contents

6: DAMNED FINE DRUMMING

About the Author

Preface

They've Packed up the Rock and Roll is both a selection of new poems and a collection of older work which, while some of it has appeared in magazines and anthologies, has never been issued in book form before.

As the title indicates, these poems reflect life experience from the twenties to the eighties. Each section represents a theme or concern in human life. "Pretty Young Brown-Eyed Ghost"—familial love; "The Harder It Becomes, the Easier It Gets"—erotic and marital love; "Prickly Ash"—the wild world; "Bare-Voiced Song"—the muse and all that; "Writing in Snow"—morality, politics, and the news; and "Damned Fine Drumming" is the last act, in every sense of that term.

There are doubtless other ways to sort out the raw experience of life as one has attempted to capture it, but this seemed appropriate to me. Within each section the work proceeds chronologically, so the progress of thought, if any, can be discerned.

I have throughout written as honestly and directly as I could, but with the sense that poetry is not after all classification or argumentation or self-revelation or music, but some of all four.

I could honestly say that *They've Packed up the Rock and Roll* is, if not my life's work—I hope there will be more beyond this— still a big important chunk of it. It's been, as we used to say when that music was new, a trip.

– Edith Rylander

These poems are dedicated to people whose help I should have
appreciated much sooner

Gertrude Stacey, third grade teacher, school librarian, Sunny-
vale Elementary School, Sunnyvale, California

Josephine Pinckney, Girl Scout Leader: Troop 1, the Lone Pine
Troop, Sunnyvale, California

Mary Smith, Journalism 1,2,3; faculty advisor to
"The Chief", Fremont Union High School,
Cupertino, California

Stanford Whitmore, creative writing teacher, Palo Alto Eve-
ning School, Palo Alto, California

Dr. Lawrence Mouat, speech and debate coach, San Jose State
College, San Jose, California

1

Pretty Young Brown Eyed Ghost

MATERNITY WARD, CATHOLIC HOSPITAL

Here where Saints Penicillin and Priapus keep
The beds from emptying, the Sisters walk,
Rustling like fields of corn midsummer deep,
When the dark earth thrusts loveliest in the stalk.
They have no traffic in that natural thrust,
The brides of Christ. Morning that brings my son
To gulp and nuzzle, brings the bell and priest,
And God on a plate, for whom the bell is rung.
(Screens bar the doors of those who do not believe.)
St. Penicillin has God up his sleeve.

My sister, in the madhouse, heard God say,
"Man's righteousness is filthy rags. Thine eye
Offends thee. Pluck it out." She ran away
To a high place, but found she could not fly.
My Baptist Jesus shriveled like green corn
In a killing frost, though it was summer then,
And songbirds on the cemetery lawn
Splashed in the sprinklers as we lowered her down.
Life is a sometime crop that comes and goes,
And what God has to do with it, God knows.

Green thrust and Priapus bring me to this bed,
To the care of Sisters with their grave kind faces,
Women well nourished by their mystical bread;
St. Penicillin cannot bridge all spaces.
The small old nun in the white habit smiles,
Corn-country German gutturals on her tongue.
"Chust all like you or me except so small—
Dey are so beautyfull, you cannot imachun."
Her white arms wrap a lifetime's newborn forms;
The great dark mother wraps us in her arms.

1967

TWO A.M. FEEDING

Here in our safe bed, in the warm valley
Between his father's back and my nursing body,
Five-week-old Eric drinks the world at my breast.

Outside, whatever the bones of Sioux and settler
Whisper in the dark of two a.m.,
Nothing moves but the easy slip of water,
Snow weeping down, worms quickening in the compost.

How did we earn this? Eric with his soft greed;
Me with the petty guilts and charities
Of thirty-two years in a well-fed country.
We have earned nothing. And though I starved myself
Till Eric cried and jerked at the limp nipple,
Those scrawny kids would shiver under bridges,
Or scream when the roof fell in a sheet of fire.
The men with the big boots would still kick doors in.
We have earned nothing. Nobody earns anything.

It will be morning soon, time to fry bacon,
Kiss people, talk about fishing, plan the garden.
The robins are back. The apple tree will flower,
However man suffers, and desires to suffer.

1967

DAN DREAMING

Lion and lamb and, for a little while, mine.
Face down among books, my literate firstborn.
What dream tonight twitches his half-grown body
As he lies sleeping?
                    Alexander of Macedon,
Red-handed dreamer, stamps the world with libraries,
Dead men, and coins.

Then there's his other "best book," a different dream;
Joseph of the Nez Perce, whose true name was Thunder
Rolling in the Mountains. His wife, called Spring of the Year,
Shot dead with their child in her lap at the fight called Big Hole;
His brother Alikut, killed in the last battle
At Snake Creek—all of them are alive,
And over the border, safe. No, not cut down
One day from Canada, like the dumb book says,
But safe, in the Queen's country. On long grass
Young laughing red boys race their spotted ponies.

Lion and lamb and for a little while mine,
Reviser of history so the Indians win,
I cannot guess his dream. Whatever I dream
For other boys, I want this one to make it
Over whatever borders he has to cross.
Let him dream the world good, oh let him like his face
In the mirrors of that world I won't survive to;

Let my child be whole at the dream's end.

                                     1968/2002

SHIREEN DREAMS HORSES

All day long, hands fumbling
At dishtowel and broom; face half-hidden
Under a hay-stack of hair.
Wherever my child is, she isn't here.

In dark the long-legged body
With the bud breasts twitches.
Bars of moonlight cross her bed,
Half illuminate her mustang pictures.

As moonlight swings open the gate, she is walking
Barefoot through crisp grass
Toward the dark grazing shapes
Which lift their heads to watch her.
Foals nuzzle her hand, mares
Sniff at her bare feet.

The stallion whickers,
The great neck bends
To the grubby, small-fingered hand.

Up. A trot. A long easy lope,
Wind taking her hair;
The dangerous gathering stride
Moving to the full gallop,
Shadow fence ticked by trailing hooves as they clear it,
Rider and ridden one in the dark.

1975

LOST CRICKETS

Along about August, crickets
Wander into the house:
Walk hesitantly across the floor
Till they find dark corners.

Looking for love, or sex, or adventure;
Whatever crickets look for in August,
They wander into the house.

Some get swatted. Some get stepped on. Some
Give their small plaintive chirp
Through sweating nights, dusty days.
Some get sucked dry by the house spiders
Who are laying eggs this time of year
And need all the nourishment they can get.

I sweep out dead crickets, black futile bundles,
Legs and ovipositors draggled with house dust,
Tangled in spiderweb, mixed up
With white spider egg sacks and leg-thrashing spiders.

When I read him *Charlotte's Web*,
My tough youngest son burst
Into furious tears at Charlotte's death.
Wilbur the pig saved Charlotte's egg sack,
But that cut no ice with Eric.
"She died!" he shouted at his mother and E.B. White.
"She died! It's not *fair!*"

This poem is sack and song in one.

Along about August, crickets
Wander into the house.

1976

IN-LAWS

My in-laws are sturdy competent women
And quiet competent men;
They let me eat their sweet rolls and marry their blood kin
As if I was every bit as good as them.

It is not their fault they were born making flawless Jello molds;
It is not their fault they are lucky as well as good;
There are no drunks in this prosperous populous family;
Nobody in this family ever went mad.

If I spend time thinking about that first, other family
It is dead waste. It has taken eighteen years
Learning to practice order, promptness, stability,
And not to spend half of my life in tears.

My sister, oh my dear, heard voices and killed herself.
Mom spent days in bed with migraine. Dad
Wrote sonnets, sang tenor, certainly drank enough.
If it all turned out like that it must have been bad.

My children do not know the songs we sang
Back then. ("Mom, when you sing that stuff you cry.")
All that is finished, that daughterhood. I am free.
The last of them all, the end of all that history.

And sometimes over the Jello molds I remember
When we ate creamed tuna on toast by candlelight
And sat at the table singing for two hours,
While the grease set up on the unwashed dinner plates.

I remember the time Dad called us from dishes, from homework;
I remember the book laid open on his thighs
That night he read "The Celestial Omnibus."
I remember his voice shook, and there were tears in his eyes.

Remembering, I am filled with fire and tears.
I do not want to be better, only to be understood.
I want to shout across the punishing years,
"It was good! It was good! It was good!"

1977

WATERING MY MOTHER-IN-LAW'S FLOWERS

The world's anonymous green voice
Raises its June carol, leaf
By leaf, blade by blade,
Joyous, perpetual, without choice;
As the oriole flashing orange
And black, stitching with light
And song the bright openings, weaving
His dangled pursed nest against
Wind and weather, sings, weaves
Generation unto generation the same;
Blind flight, Panama to Minnesota,
Crying "teacher teacher" to leaves.

Against which rises the voice
Of Elsie's flowerbeds; rows, curves,
Mum buds pinched back
For more bloom, weeds repulsed
And bugs squashed: ordered like a ballet
Or a farmhouse pantry. A place for everything.
Petunias in a barrel, impatiens in a bowl,
Planned, planted, set out to stay
That great green flood and tumble
Which would have it all weed and brush
In two months, woods in two years,
"Teacher teacher" cried to jungle.

Against, yet part, as falling water
Shapes gravity's curve; as in the orchestra
The soloist lifts the violin; wood,
Gut, hair, meat and bone, partner
And part of the glad noise life
Makes living. Blood-thump, breath-rush,

Yet apart, saying, singing,
"I am I, I am earth
Made conscious and particular, alone
Above the tide of sound, improvising
On a known theme, reverent
But curious, carrying on
Beauty, harmony, into the unknown.

1977

MY MOTHER'S PAIN

My mother's pain, about which I can do nothing,
Clenches down into my head like claws, till I crawl
Out of my husband's arms for aspirin.

She says, in her letter, written in 1980,
That I made her a promise in 1959
Which I broke in '63, and don't remember.
Clearly, clearly, I do not love her enough.

She is widowed and poor, tormented by her own demons,
Her one living child half a country
And half a life away from her.
And when she wrote those words, she could not bear her life.

Time, fate, those near deaths bear down on her,
Taking away the woman she once was,
Her songs, her joy, her dancing.
If I loved her enough, somehow I could make her whole,
Because, as she taught me, love can cure everything.

In my dark far house with my children safe in their beds,
I slip back into the bed where my husband
Sleeps his dear uncomplicated sleep.
I pour out love with all the force of my being,
And it's never enough. It's never, never enough.

1980-2017

PSYCH WARD

Now as I talk to these people, sign these papers,
I remember I was one of the world's great criers.
I sit here calm-faced, watching the sun glare
Off a drab-painted wall.
                              Where are the tears
I gave to Keats, and the Joads, and my Dad's harmony,
And Frodo Baggins, and little kids in commercials?
She clings and clings to me, who is as far from me
In the orbit of her mind as those strange stars
Which fall in on themselves and give no light,
Their gravity being beyond what we even dream;
We easy criers, we cheerful junkies of hope.
I will walk off down that hall past those doors and that bright
Poster for exercise class. I will not scream.
If I start crying now, I will never stop.

1981

FOR A SEVENTY-FIFTH BIRTHDAY
For my Mother-in-Law

Sometimes a person feels like it's just not worth it;
The dust comes back on the furniture, the weeds
Come back in the garden. The work gets harder.
The kids grow up and go off
And do these crazy things, and the grandchildren—
(Those hairy, lippy rock-and-rollers)
Sometimes a person really doesn't want to know,
But worries. And people you love get sick
And die, and wherever they are then
Is a long way off from you, with no talking
Across that gap.

Meanwhile, in the middle of the woods
Are the flowers; in the middle of the hurt,
Of the wars, of the dirt, of the craziness, is a place
Of quiet and order, and a table
Nobody goes home hungry from. Here there is the kind of laughter
That never hurt anybody. Here is Elsie's house.
Here is love. Here is prayer.

When the owner goes and never comes back, when the spirit's house
Is empty, we will remember light and order,
And charity which suffereth long.
We will pick up the tools we had dropped
And stand a little straighter:
We will keep on.

1981

GRIEF WORK

Often enough before
I've dreamed this stupid dream;
The dullest of dull housework
To be done over and over.

Though some corner of my brain
Knows it's a dream, and tells me,
"Wake up, woman, get it over!"
The dream takes its own time.

This is another dream;
The big old house I am dreaming
Is almost the house where my husband
Lived once with his mother Elsie,

Whom I helped care for last winter
When she lay slowly dying;
Clothing, books, dishes, letters,
These are Elsie's things I am sorting

With a group of other women,
Some sisters-in-law, some strangers,
All of us ordering after the fact
Her seventy-seven years.

This dream too is endless,
This putting away in boxes
What loved hands lovingly tended—
Elsie, come back, walk through the door,

Let your laugh grounded in gardens,
Your strong Swede voice go sweeping
Away and away these cobwebs!
Then we'll sit and talk and drink coffee,

And walk spring woods together
Among the first hepaticas.—
I am awake in my own bed;
Chickadees sing for morning.

And up the hill in an empty house
All Elsie's stuff needs sorting.
Time for breakfast and coffee.
Time for starting over.

1984

TALKING TO RICK

Over the phone you sound just the same.
Same hip-kid-from-the-Mission-district bite
As you lift the ends of words,
Though it's kids we're talking, yours, mine—

There you are in the Christmas picture,
Square-faced, big bellied, a regular burgher
In front of the split-level, arm around the wife—

My city cousin, who taught me a thing or two.

Last time I saw you was in '70.
Dad was dying. Back from the hospital
We stood around in the kitchen,
Drinking bourbon and jive-talking
As if we owned stock in the year 1952,
When I was dateless and friendless,
When your friends were starting heroin.

Now Pacific Gas and Electric
Is paying you good money
For your wrecked back,
And my youngest kid
Runs around in black leather and chains.

I wouldn't be young again if you paid me,
But just for a minute
I slide down your voice into the '49 Merc,
Tailpipes and neon, California freeway,
And the crackly radio pumping out "One Bad Stud."

1985

ODDS AND ENDS

Elsie, we're doing the last little bit of cleaning,
Getting your house ready to sell.

The rooms that were full of furniture, the shelves that were full of food,
The closets that were full of clothes are empty;
Nothing is left but odds and ends.

Old bulletins from your church.
Cotton dresses with garden stains
And balled Kleenex in the pockets.

On the wooded slope the hepaticas
Have bloomed twice since you saw them;
Six-petaled tiny flowers, white, pink, blue, lavender,
Blown and done.

Among the green-gold lace of buds and tiny leaves
The just-back birds who move too fast
To be sure of their names bounce and flutter
And cry from high twigs, "Look quick! Look quick!

Look!"

1985

LETTER TO THE FIRST BORN

Kept dreaming about you all night long,
Every dream more depressing than the last,
Though in the dreams, at least you were coming home
Like you used to. Old wreck cars rumbling
Into the driveway, you
Skinny as a weasel, hungry as if
You hadn't had a decent meal in weeks,
Thundering in on a wave of rock and roll,
Your duffle-bag full of funky socks.

Toward dawn, reality
Sipping in on whiffs of coffee,
You added heft, subtracted hair, became
That thirty-plus man we never get news from.

Yeah, this is the usual whine for maternal access,
As if I'd never had those publications,
Was just some sinkbound whimperer, poor Mom.
Listen, kid; I get along fine without you.

We both remember that Viking-bearded boy
Took a few wounds, and scared the living beJesus
Out of the old folks more times than a few,
Trying on lots of stuff I had no time for,
Back in my slim days, tending you—
The firstborn wear the glow of pure potential,
Sweet as their birthbloom, and about as lasting.

So: how's it going? Good luck on those tests.

I keep sending sass and bruises, when I wish
I could send some charm: some sword, some healing magic,

That would call every bird of the sky down to your aid,
When you are lost and bruised and sore afraid.

I send what I have in the envelope of my years.
The taste of home-made bread fresh from the oven;
Wood smoke smells and chain saw whines and the
nose tang
Of wet wool and freezing sheep shit,
And cut alfalfa curing in June sun.
The ticks and pops of wood heat, and soft laughter
Behind closed doors.
The rain clatter
Of the typewriter late at night.

1990

FAMILY STORIES

I: GRANDMA EDITH TOLD ME

When Grandma Edith told me that family history,
We were ladies, we were gentlemen, we had lived,
Or might have lived, or ought to have lived, in castles.
To this day some of the Oregon descendants
Are tracing dubious lines to deflated kings.

And we were heroes for God:
Pastors, evangelists, men who left the plow
In the fields, God having spoken direct
Into their heads. Men who told the wife,
"Pack the clothes and call the children home.
We are going out into the world to preach the Gospel,
Bringing the word of God to the unsaved."
And those wives obeyed.

Considering actual lives
Of people I loved and knew
Reminds me of college textbooks,
Checklists for social workers.
Old pains, old stews of grievance;
That bitter porridge eaten by the cheated
From generation to generation,
Passed on to the kids.
Chronicles of crazies, drunks, and Welfare mothers,
People worn down by life.

And when God spoke direct
Into my sister's head,
He told her she had to die,
Which she promptly did.

Grandma would say it is the style
With which adversity is born
That makes a life more than animal scramble.
The elegance of a table setting, the possession
Of a library card.
All these gestures that separated us
From the common people,
Most of them in the other branch
Of my family tree.
The dust on God's feet, the world's trash.

2006

II: ANNIVERSARY DREAMS

It was not exactly you
In last night's dream
Which I can't even clearly remember.
It was death, though;
It was sure enough death.

I never thought of you once
All yesterday, as he and I exchanged cards,
Shopped, talked, laughed, ate lobster,
Went home and made love,
Glad for our thirty-eight years
As husband and wife.

Though I do not forget, ever
That first wedding anniversary
On which, by bitter chance
Of hallucination and the law of gravity
We buried you.

I know you would not choose
Bad dreams for your big sister,
Anymore than you chose
That the firework of your life
Should rain burns on the upturned faces
Of those who loved you best;
Mother, father, husband, child
Who does not remember you,
Or the grandkids you never knew.

In your right mind you were kind.

In all these years, remembering you

I have eaten and drunk and loved
With double appetite,
As if I could send it to you,
Music and wine and sun
Across the great dark.

Be in my dreams when you choose
As half-heard voice, or corpse,
Or girl in the cashmere skirt
In which we buried you,
Half-glimpsed at a dream party,
Casually turning away.

You who were childhood playmate
And teenaged dancing partner,
Dead now for longer
Than you had time to live,
Be with me in my age,
Pretty young brown-eyed ghost.

2006

III: WEEDING THE ONIONS

"Most men lead lives of quiet desperation."
When I first read that line in Thoreau
I thought, "Yeah! Yeah!"
And swore I could do better,

And it never occurred to me
That keeping your desperation to yourself
Is preferable to visiting it on your neighbors.
Even noisy desperation is better
Than rape, nerve gas, killing—serial or mass—
The things humans do
When life wears them down.

Young, I was promised the ecstasy of God
If I would surrender my whole soul.
But the price seems high,
And I can't turn off the news.

I kneel to no known God
In the damp dirt of the onion patch,
And pull what needs pulling,
My mind losing its griefs, filling slowly
With small animal words.
Smell. Taste. Ache. Hunger.
Sky. Dirt.
Sleep.

2006

THE GIFT

"When I was a little older than you," he tells them,
"I worked all summer on my uncle's thrash rig."

"Listen to your grandfather," says their mother,
And they do, mostly, but with confusion in their eyes.
What is a thrash rig? And is Grandpa
Finding fault with their softer summers?

He reaches across time to give them his summers.
Not just as history, a thing said.
He wants to pour his memories into them:

The wakings in pre-dawn dark, the clanks and smells and bounces
That jolted him back from dozing in his uncle's workworn truck,
As they drove empty roads to today's farm,
To the big breakfast at the full farmhouse table.

The 1940s, that was. Young men mostly taken by the war.
So, just turned fifteen, youngest of the guys,
He walked out to Uncle Louie's threshing machine
Standing in first light,
Monumental on a mown field.

He was part, all day, of the roar and clatter,
Of every moment his body and hands busy,
As the flow of grain poured in,
Wagonloads drawn by tractors or horses,
A golden flood pitched unceasingly
Onto the belt that took it into the Moline,
Which spit out separate streams of oats and straw.

That first summer he was a bagger,
Catching that golden stream.
He shows them, his hands remembering,
Exactly the motion to fill, to tie off, to lift.
(He has a bag like that at home now,
Which they have seen, not knowing what it was.
Now they will know, now that he has shown them.)
Next summer, older, stronger,
He was a spiker, pitching the bundled grain on.

All day the work, save for brief moments of rest
When the machine clogged up, and his God-fearing uncle
Crawled into its hot and dusty guts
To unstick things, and curse.

Those summers burn in him now. The light moving,
The dews of morning burning off. The noon dinner
Back at the farmhouse,
A big meal cooked on a woodstove in the heat.
A breath, a chance to sit down, a little talk,
Than the walk back
For the heavy blazing afternoons, the slow downslope toward dusk.

The sharp or laughing voices yelling over the noise of the rig,
The whinny of a young horse
Frightened by the grain-eating monster.
The smells: grass, oats, machine oil, dust,
Hot iron, sweat of men and horses.

The feeling of hands and body
Pushed past ease or comfort.

Then, at last, time for the truck, for the ride home,
Itching with dirt, too tired almost to talk,
Dead tired, but proud,

Having done a man's job, having earned a day's pay,
Having been part, even,
Of feeding a hungry nation that was at war.
So ready for bed, but knowing tomorrow
Would bring in harvest on another farm.

Seventy years gone. This man needs
To give his memories to these boys
Who carry his seed into their different world.
They may not think they need to know this now,
But in due time they will need to know these things.

So he leans forward and begins again,
"When I was a little older than you—"

2015

PASSING THROUGH

Sunday morning. I tune the radio
To my news and culture station,
And out of the tangle of sounds
An old hymn leaps into me,

And I'm eight or nine, in church,
Pleased that we will get to sing
A hymn with some zip to it,
Despite its doleful words.

"This world is not my home,
I'm just a-passin' through—"
How deeply at home I am
In my Sunday dress and shoes,

In this place warm
With Jesus' nurturing love,
With Mom, with Dad,
With Grandma, with my sister.

Mom's clear soprano, Dad's tenor,
Grandma's voice, a little rusty,
But still the voice of a preacher's child,
And Joy and I, with our earnest pipings,

Singing, "Oh Lord, oh Lord,
I have no friend but you.
If heaven's not my home,
Then, Lord, what will I do?"

Of course, heaven would be our home,
But first there was church, then the ride
In our boxy little car
To our house where nothing bad had happened yet,

To, maybe, after lunch, a board game,
Or a country drive, all singing,
"The angels beckon me
From heaven's open door—"

And how could I have been
More at home in this world,
In my undamaged body,
In my untested life?

I look back seventy-plus years, and I am
Wholly at home in this world,
Everybody else gone.
The angels who beckoned them

Were cancer, stroke, and suicide.
I don't believe a word of this hymn.
I don't miss Jesus, who was once so real to me.
I miss them, knowing

This world is nobody's home,
But it's the best we've got.
They were just passing through. I'm still here.
Sunday morning, and I sing for them.

2015

BURNING MY SISTER'S PINCUSHION

We remain in the world while memory endures.

I remember when Joy made that maternity smock.
Spring-green fabric with a sheen on it.
She took my hand and laid it
Over the curve of her belly.
I felt her child moving under that cloth.

I remember her crisp brown hair, her way of talking,
Dance moves she taught me, songs we heard together.

Out of the scraps left after she made the smock
She made an embroidered bib,
And a pincushion, this little hillock of green.

After the madness, after the suicide,
There was little enough.
I got a few books with her handwriting in them,
("Write me one someday, kid!");
The set of canisters I'd given her when she married,
Three refrigerator dishes—I dropped and broke the bigger one—
And her pincushion.

I used the pincushion for years, but now
It won't hold a pin anymore;
A shapeless lump full of old punctures, not even green.

When they sort my things, my children will ask,
"Why on earth did Mom hang onto this?"
And smother that helpless laughter
Which sometimes follows a death.

No laughter, ever, for her death,
But memory endures when stuff falls apart.
I can't stand to put it in the trash, I lay it
Next to the red coals of the fire
That warms our house.
No time for ceremony. One puff and it's gone
As if it had never been.

And I feel the lighter for that burning.
Except that it was touched
By her real, her living skin,
And the bones that would have done for a long lifetime.

Three people are left in the world
Who were touched by those hands.
The child who kicked under that smock,
To whom her mother can only be
The faintest of ghosts, a memory in the bones.
And her husband, so young then,
So hurt, so bewildered, so lost
Who has made another life with its own griefs since.

I still feel her hand, smaller than mine, wholly trusting.
("You're the big sister, you take care of Joy.")
Mama would send us out to play.
We ran,
We ran out into the world, her shorter legs
Stretching to match mine.

At three, at five, some of the places we went
Were a bit steep for those legs.
I would give a yank to hoist her up,
And up she would fly like thistledown,
Laughing, agile and fearless,
Running away, leaving me in her dust.

2016

SAME HOSPITAL, FORTY-NINE YEARS LATER

Back then I was in the maternity ward,
All masonry and mystery; nuns
Sailing by, their robes trailing,

And at six a.m. the decisive stride
Of the priest coming down the hall,
Muttering, "Body of Christ, Body of Christ."

I was falling asleep after nursing,
After that lovely little face at my breast,
That mouth just learning the world;
Then he had to go back to the nursery.
The footsteps got nearer,
The nurse did something at my room-mate's bed,
Then whipped a paper doily down on my chest,
Glanced at the name-plate over my head
Where they list "religion," asked me, "Do you wish to Partake?"
I was baffled, but shook my head,

And she whipped away the doily.
The room-mate had just born her seventh;
The priest thrust God into her face
Just as she was, half-asleep in her split-tailed gown.
With no chance to order her hair or thoughts, she Partook.

This trip I am in the Heart and Vascular Center,
All angles, glass, polished granite,
Young nurses in pastel scrubs.
And forms, forms, forms,
Waiting, more forms, anxiety pushed aside,
Mouth parched, fasting since midnight.

43

Then all of a sudden things happened!
Stuff was stuck onto me, the IV went into the elbow's bend,
The big jovial anesthetist wheeled me
Off down the hall fast, saying,
"I'll be your bartender this trip!"
Then something hot zipped into my arm, and I was gone.

In due time I was in a nice big room

With my husband, and a dinky couch where he slept,
And a great view of the Mississippi
Which neither of us was in shape to enjoy.

A long night then. Nurses constantly asking,
"How do you feel?" The hardware tugged
At my skin, the blood pressure cuff
Squeezed and let go and squeezed,
And the place in the upper chest
Where the pacemaker went in ached, ached.

This morning, no baby, no priest,
No time for hair or dentures
As they bundled me into the wheelchair
To meet not God, but the X-ray;
At the door of the room my cardiologist
Looms in front of me, booms, "Hello!"
Whips open the top of my robe,
Looks at my wound, says loudly, "Great!"
And is off down the hall to check another customer.

When I'm back my husband brings coffee
From the lounge. He's passed an open door.
Man propped up in bed, wife sitting beside him,
Man saying loudly, firmly,
"I'm alive! I'm fine!"

The coffee smells wonderful, but the nurse cries, "No!"
You can't have anything yet! We haven't seen the X-rays!
We may have to go back in!"

So we wait, we wait. "Back in!"
Rings in our ears. But at last, at last
I am allowed to bundle, one-armed and clumsy
Into proper grown-up clothes,
Then back into the wheelchair
And I'm sailing down the hall to home, home!

Forty-nine years ago I went home
Holding my son wrapped
In his grandmother's crocheted blanket,
Blue eyes blinking at the winter sun,
The world's first wind on his face.

Others are entering as I leave,
Or making the trip home, like me,
Holding in my arms the monitor
To read the little engine in my chest.

We wave to each other,
We are not new and beautiful,
But as the old boy said from his bed, "Alive!"
And almost, maybe, pretty soon now, well.

2017

DANCING QUEEN

As we wait in the outer office at the vitreoretinal clinic,
Somebody behind us whistles a snatch of "Dancing Queen,"
And I remember my daughter, at thirteen,
Listening to that tune whenever it came on the radio,
Catching each word, writing it down in green ink, every "Oh yeah,"

"She is the dancing queen, young and sweet, only seventeen."

She was so often angry then, at the great chasm
Between scruffy too-young thirteen,
And what the world might give her, at seventeen.

I can't identify the whistler, and it's our turn.
Slim blonde Dr. Polly, with four kids, and a magic needle
Full of vision-saving medicine,
With which she'll pierce, yet again,
My husband's well-loved eyes.

"That pressure's a little higher than we'd like, John;
Try this new eye-drop. I'll want to check that.
Can you come back Monday?"

It's an hour's drive, but of course we come back Monday.
The girl with the green ink
Will want to know how this went;
She has her own teens now, but
She stays in touch;
Scolds us when we do too much.

The whistler's version was slower
Than those lilting, dance-floor Swedes,

A meditation on ourselves, as our calendars
Fill with clinic visits.

Somebody recalled that tune
As they waited for the needle.
Age is no barrier
In the heart of dancing queens.

2017

2

The Harder It Becomes, The Easier It Gets

THAT I GO FROM HIM SHINING
Poems for John: Eight

Know, know that when I go from you
I walk down streets made out of gold,
I burn and shine and sing with you,
And bright uncatchable birds fly wild.

The thistles groan with golden apples
And blossoms burst out of the stones
Where the light from me shifts and dapples;
And all the geese turn into swans.

1958

GREENNESS

It does no good dreaming of that green time
Before Adam made his forays among leaves;
Before the flaming sword, the broken bottle,
The wayside boulder daubed with "Jesus Saves."

Even when Sieur DuLuth made marriages
Between his company and the Dakota girls,
A man could take his woman among greenness
With nobody minding what they did but squirrels.

Civil amorists take greenness where they can;
I praise those parks where we have paid our dollar
For tent-space, fifteen trees, a strip of sky.
There was one camp, a valley in California

Where a slow river gurgled in warm June dark,
And bullfrogs grunted like a choir of satyrs.
You over me and dew-smelling crushed grass under,
And the night sky over your shoulder, spawning stars.

Suppose some ranger, some nice young man
Had taken us coupling on his state-owned greensward?
Could we have shown him the ring, the teaching contract,
The well-adjusted sleeping two-year-old

Tucked up in the tent? I see him point like Jehovah,
Exiling Eve for traffic with the snake.
He was hired to keep that freedom safe for frogs.
Civilization is not a choice you make.

1962

NIGHT BEGAN WITH YOUR VENTURING

Night began with your venturing
Into my alien darkness, going that journey
Blood-naked, driving in through shuddering freshets,
Mauled and gnawed in the rapids of my need,
Till you shuddered and cried and all you had poured into me.

Howls yanked me from sleep. It was four a.m.
I made room in the bed for Eric's three-month mouth,
Absurd legs, damp belly against my body
That smelled of man-stuff. Sticky at the thighs
From your pouring-out, I felt the sweet ache of milk
Coming down. My son took life at my breast.

1967

POEMS FOR JOHN: 220

Even for this wordless speech of our meeting bodies
There are literary formulas; you can list positions,
Transcribe gasps, describe moonlight on bare shoulders,
Or the car passing the house in a spatter of gravel.

Once we found that treetop flyer the scarlet tanager,
Dark wings intact, red body brilliant on gravel,
With no ants busy yet at the shut eyes.

Words for the wordless marrying of our bodies
Are the body of the tanager, not the tanager.

1969

BONES

I think even the skeleton, the dry bone
Will show what you were. As in the room you built me.
Choosing the trees yourself, cutting them yourself,
Sawing, drying, nailing into place board by careful board,
Unpainted, with only a sealer. Red oak, black ash, birch,
Every grain itself.

                  Whatever grass they lie in,
Your bones will say John, in the empty eye-hole,
In the done marrow.

                  Most paint everything, walls, memories,
Not you.

              Poems will grab their shoulders
And shake them, and a wind of words
Like leaves on a live bough shaking will shout them down, shouting
"Remember, remember!" Keeping you, the quick
Alive push of blood under skin, the pulse at the throat,
(Leaves over boughs, grass over done bone)
Laughter in a room, you in bright sun,
Shifting of shadows on your skin, leaf shadows,
You laughing, you touching me deep, you pulling me down

                  Where everything goes.

Somebody will find a crumpled half-leaf
Of poetry in a dead language.
And your bones whisper like the rest as the wind goes through them,
"I walked, I ate and drank, I looked at the sun, and got children.
A girl loved me once. Now she's dead too."

                        1969

FORNICATION, A CERTAIN GOOD

"All our ideas are death oriented…If I were twenty I
would fornicate and take drugs against this terrible strain
of idiots who govern the world…Fornication, at least that
is something good."
Albert Szent-Gyorgi, Noble laureate, discoverer of Vitamin C

I slide easily from morning dream
To morning reality, in a high bright room.
Fingers twitch my nipples awake. Lips nuzzle my back. Lower,
A stir and rising.

A certain good; satiny flesh like risen bread.
Hard blood thrusting under my touch.
My inner flesh moves
As if to swallow.

Enough this is enough slide, twist, and supple counterthrust
          Age cannot wither you nor custom stale
          Your infinite variety
World, do your worst Twelve years come July I've had this
What if the world starves, if the sea dies, if the sky chokes us,
If this is last and forever
As I turn crying, caught

And it's over.
We curl together a moment
While the waking children chatter like squirrels
In the house below.

He dresses quickly,
Smooths down his hair with one sweep of his hand,
Clatters downstairs. I watch from the window
As he strides toward the dog kennels through February snow.

Fond, like Szent-Gyorgyi,
Of "children, the ocean, wild-life, Bach."
Brown eyes and laughing mouth
Under the soft mustache.
Going to give the dogs their morning walk.

1970

SUBLIMATION

When Keats and Shakespeare were desperately hard up,
They didn't prowl around the house muttering darkly,
"Everybody's getting it but me."
They wrote, "The expense of spirit," "St. Agnes' Eve,"
And "La Belle Dame Sans Merci."

At least that's true if you go with Sigmund and Company,
Whom I picture as stroking gray, luxurious beards,
Well past the age of sexual urgency.
They must all have been better at sublimation than me.

Because how, for God's sake, does a person write anything,
Feeling iron stays tightening around her belly?
Metaphor and dishes slithering from thick hands,
Unable to speak sensibly or breathe deeply?
Pacing as men with a bad conscience do,
Or caged-up cougars in a small-town zoo.

The white-sailed frigates of rationality
Split on these stones. "He's tired." "It's those faculty meetings."
"It's only been three days." Split and go under,
Weltering in that salt estranging sea.
"Oh God, I want him and he doesn't want me."

Afterwards—yes, anything is possible.
The deep-sea keel rocking in gentle haven
Its nets all silver with miraculous scales.
The long swells breaking, the flight of sun-touched birds.
I make this poem in an afterwards.

1972

AUGUST

Heat pressing down
On haymow and hill.
The house dug in
To the hill slope, surrounded
By the woods its wood came from.

What I've come down to;
Picking corn in the seminal perfume
Of crisping corn-silk. Sweat in my eyes
As I bend to the floor of the coop, hens squawking,
Gathering breakfast in the shell,

I grew up in those houses
Flown from the architect's brain and the ready pen
Of the financier.
No beam in them grown there, shooting up
Like dreams in the downed orchards
Of California. Sung to
By cement-lined ravines with the names of rivers;
Sung to all night by a river of wheels, the stud
Cruising for chicks, the roar of the long-haul trucker.

We work together, man and wife. Under the trees in front of the woodshed,
We plunge just-killed chickens into hot water. Strip plumage,
Carry future dinners
Downstairs, into basement cool, cutting and gutting and bagging,
And stacking away for winter in the freezer.

Chicken-guts go into the compost bin
Next to the out-house. Shovel on dirt.
Scrub blood from under the nails. Fry chicken

For dinner. Go down
Into cool darkness, couple
In smells of dust and summer.
Wind through the trees touches the wet places.

1978

THE EASIER IT GETS, THE HARDER IT BECOMES:
THE HARDER IT BECOMES, THE EASIER IT GETS
For John: February 14, 1980

Knocked off our feet, ass over teakettle, tumbled
And sliding in sweet green, oh leaf, frond, slither and glide
Down that immortal slope, grass-stained, pollen-smeared,
Lovely, light, leafy, easy, easy—

But soon enough down to the hard stuff, grit, crack-bone gravel,
Bedrock and bone, the long thrum
Of blood by blood, shifting strata
Of burned-out stars, fire under the eyelids, dark,
Dark again, sweet rush and crumble,
Mold, mould.
                    Holding
In clenched flesh a river of seed, a comet of making
And being made, each grinding in, root into stone,
Deep, deep.

Now stand hard against cold sky
The clean bare branches. Wholly without pretense
The bare dear architecture of twenty-one years,
Form following function.

There is a long wind coming from far off
Wears us by little and little. Crumbs of forever
Tumble and tumble down.

(At twenty-four I dreamed we were old, gray, frail,
Beyond love's thrust, holding then each the other,
In gray stick arms and saying, "Do you remember?")

Tumble and tumble down, wind-searched, spread, sifted,
Dark, waiting, dumb.

Slime-mould and fairy dust, epithelium,
Seed in the wind.

1980

PLANTING IN DRIZZLE, MAY

Planting in drizzle. May.
Use the pine-board row spacer so the rows
Are far enough apart to run the tiller.
Line out straight with poles and string.
This end of the garden, heavy soil with a tinge of red to it;
The middle section black loam, the end
Loam with a little sand.

Finish out the row of transplanted lettuces
With radish and endive.
Dark heavy soil furrowed with the pointed hoe.
Fat worms. Nine years' manure and compost.
Pull out snaky roots of quack grass.
Shirt getting a little wet.

Now a double row of parsnips to overwinter
And harvest after next year's snow.
Papery beige seeds like small eyes
In the narrow groove. Crumble soil over
And tramp firm, heel and toe with feet.

Killdee, killdee, a killdeer circling and calling
In the fine rain. Maybe the same bird
Who nested last year in the corn field,
Doing the broken wing trick, drawing
Us off from her little ones,
So nearly invisible on the earth.

Bend and stress of the body.
Damp dirty clothes, damp fingers
Sprinkling seed, sprinkling dirt over.
The mind jumping around, spurting out sentences,

Then words, then hanging
On one word or two like a refrain.
The mind emptying. The mind filling
With wet and seed-feel,
Cry of birds in the rain.

Raining harder. Put poles and string and hammer
Back where they came from.
Hang up the hoe on the outhouse wall.

1982

SPLITTING WOOD

1. FIND THE BALANCE POINT

Stand the chunk on its base so it doesn't wobble;
Find the balance point.
(John's voice giving instruction,
Though he's off in the woods with tractor and chain saw
Getting another load.)

There. Get a good grip.
Stand level, legs apart.
Swing blade edge first, *thunk!*

The chunk hops away.
Hit it square, don't tie your body up, use that muscle!
Chop with the blade, not the handle!

I'll never get as good at this
As John or the boys,
To stand the chunk up and swing
All in one easy motion,
Cloven eighths and quarters,
Falling easy as bright leaves,
Clean dry good-smelling wood
For the winter stoves.

But I've learned the rest, learned
By feel and look and smell
Fast-burning basswood, smoldering maple,
From hard, coal-forming oak and elm.

Stacked cut wood in the trailer, ridden
High and bumping, throned

On what I gathered and stacked,
Lurching through mist or under bright fall skies,
Arms scratched with prickly ash, ducking face-slap branches,
Sweating. And pleased with myself.

Unloaded it all
And stacked it in the woodshed.
(Nothing corrects a careless stacker
Like a rank of wood rumbling down,
A shin banger that could have cracked a skull.)

And after the splitting,
Hauled it in by armloads,
Made the woodstove sing
With sweet heat and smells of supper.

High time I learned to split my own kindling.
Set the chunk level.
Find the balance point.

1985

2. STRENGTH THROUGH WEAKNESS

Like all my gender generation,
I was taught weakness, gentleness,
Sweetness, niceness;

To run a hundred yards
And give up, fluttering;
To view thrown balls
As face-smashing missiles,
To melt into helplessness
In the presence of a male.

Carefree hair
Stiffened with lacquer,
Open smile
Stiffened with niceness,

To win by losing, to seduce
(Nicely! Nicely!)
Some Big Lug of a Nice Boy
Into taking care of me forever!

I grab with the hand, I set the chunk
On its base, I spread my legs, I swing
With the biting ax whose blade
Could gash me to the bone.

Wife of one, mother of three,
Learning at fifty to run,
Taking the ax in hand,
Doing my own cutting.

1985

3. DOING THINGS FOR YOU

My mother used to click her tongue and sigh
Over those poor relations whose husbands
Kept them in wood-heated shanties
With outhouses;
She's too nice to say it, but she thinks I'm crazy,
Hauling block and mixing mortar
For the composting outhouse.

Fourth of July at the lake cottage.
Humid, high eighties. Mother Rylander, heavy, near seventy,
Took the water buckets downhill to the pump.
Filled them and lugged them back uphill
Alone, though the house
Was full of strong daughters and strapping grandsons:
"Oh, you should have let us help you!"

Set down her buckets with a thump.
"You let people start doing things for you,
And pretty soon you can't do them for yourself."

1985

4. S.L.O.L.

I'll dig in, I'll get old
Like a denned bear,
Or a wolf gone off to die,
Like that old Finn who hanged himself
The day he couldn't split the family kindling.

Would I leave my kids that?

But if I keep the ax sharp they won't get me,
Smothering with kindness, "Mom, it's nice there—"

Time may yet make me
A Sweet Little Old Lady like all the other S.L.O.L's,
Eating the same nice food, watching the same nice game shows,
Listening to the same nice music. Preachers and central heating!
No more prickly ash, no rock and roll.

That tough old German in the nursing home
Where my daughter worked when she was sixteen;
Parading down the hall buck naked,
Shriveled old privates out,
Pissing in the sheet sterilizer,

Blocking the doors of his room
So they had to break in on him,
To find him sitting in mussed bedclothes,
Old tangle of skin and bones and white hair,

Yanking out his I.V.'s, moaning,
"I just want to live my own life!"
He wasn't dying. He was healing. The treatment he hated

Got him well and sent him home.
He clipped my girl in the face with a boot.
Even fighting to live his own life,
A mean old bastard is a mean old bastard.

1985-2018

5. VARIOUS DEATHS

Trees die deaths as various
As their height and shape,
Leaf-hue, life-span;
Quick-dying birch, eight-hundred-year-old white oak,
Thousand or three
Of the redwoods, bristlecone pine
Just goes on cloning.

But the bug or virus comes,
Or windstorm, or lightning,
Maybe a scream of torn fiber
And a thundering crash.

Nothing goes down
With the grace of a tree;
Bushels of leaves
Blending into other leaves,
Trunk all riddled with woodpecker holes
And squirrel hideouts,
Oyster mushroom in succulent brackets
All full of little beetles;
All those cleansing and rendering lives,
Bacteria, fungi, ferns;

The roothole
Becoming a den, then rounding
Into a small cupped hollow,
The downed trunk softening
Into a green ridge of humus,
Old forest floors patterned with hollows and ridges
That were trees once.

So let me go down
When I come to term,
Cells powdering into leaf-mold, fluids
Trotting off in the bodies of bugs,
Life structure hanging a little while
On the retina of the mind.
The world enriched, marked faintly
With hollow and ridge.

1985

6. A MAN WITH CONFIDENCE

Set the chunk on its base, thunk!
Ax sticks. But another swing or two
Splits the wood. Kindling falls.
Not regular or perfect, but it all burns.

And the tractor
Rumbles in with another load.
John shuts the engine off, climbs down, walks over,
Knocking bark and sawdust off his clothes;
Weathered face, twig in his beard, smiling:

A man with confidence enough
To put an ax into his wife's hands.

1985

FIFTEEN YEARS

The first four inches
The trowel slips in easy.
Fifteen years' compost.

At the depth of the trowel blade
The work gets hard.
The clay of the worked-over field
This was when we started.
Clay over glacier scrapings,
The world's flinty bones.

1984

MESSAGE ENCLOSED IN A WALL
IN A HOUSE CALLED "EARTHWARD"

Whoever you are,
Archeologist or wrecker,
Here are some words from 1988,
Written on the fifth of February
With the thermometer well below zero,
And the sun bright on drifted snow
In the woods around this house
Which we named for our compulsions
And a poem by Robert Frost.
(American poet, 1874-1963.)

This house buried in earth,
With its exposed beams, south-facing windows,
And walls of cordwood masonry,
Was not typical of its time and region,
Nor can the builders who lived in it
Be taken as a baseline norm.
We were teacher and poet;
We had raised three children before we built this place.
We built as much as we could
With our own hands.

We cut the trees for this house,
We gathered its stones
From the worked-over country
Of a place called Minnesota.
Half-expecting the nuclear death of everything
At the hands of our own species,
We built as we could.

(As I write this, my husband is waiting
With the finishing trowel in his hand.)

Listen. As you take the old paper
Out of the old bottle, out of this wall
We dreamed and sweated,
Our message is, we were homo sapiens.
We loved each other thirty years.
When we made something, we cleaned up after ourselves.

1988

YOUR 54th VALENTINE

You would think after all this time together
I would remember February 14 th a little better,
And not be stuck, at greeting-card-appropriate times,
With homemade rhymes.

This year, hoping not to fail at this simple marital duty,
I looked upon the Hallmark rack in its seasonal beauty,
And, amidst all that goo and fluff,
Could not find anything strong enough, true enough,
For this long saga of our being together.

This will be another of my kitchen-scribbled tunes,
Like the valentine that compared love to a glacier, or the couplet
Written on a sticky note, stuck on a box of prunes.

We wait, hand in hand, for what time has in store.
We love as best we can. We can do no more.

February 14 th , 2013

3

Prickly Ash

TREES

That year, in everything we did there were trees.
The light we woke to, mornings when loons chattered
Over the lake, came filtered through basswood leaves
Moving in wind. There were slivers under our nails.

With fall we cut wood, stacked wood, split wood, burned wood,
Learned wood by heft in the hand and the smell of smoke
And the color of flame. Turning, half asleep,
I could tell by the deeper roar when the backlog took hold.
We made love with the incense of birch or slippery elm bite
Caught in our hair, scenting each pore of our skin.

All useless knowledge. That wood's not ours to sell
If we wanted to sell it. No one buys learned articles
On heating with wood, its practice and aesthetic.

It's like that other skill. Suppose I could dance
On my back as eloquently as Cleopatra?
My husband had trust enough to marry me virgin,
Will never be rich, and could not love me more.

White basswood is good for a quick fire, and light in the hand.
I have that much of the world in my bone-marrow;
I have that joy of knowing and being known.

1965

ROBINS

At the end of April there were two whole days
When the hill behind our cabin was full of robins.
Migrating, probably, to other nest sites.
Stopping to feed, with a little courting thrown in.

Shaking rugs or going out to the privy,
We heard them. Detached bright notes
Falling in the stillness. Any movement at all
Among the naked trees or over the brown dead leaves
Wet with runoff, was robins, bright-breasted robins.

Well, and suppose we did; suppose we managed
The arrangements of a lifetime to put us there
In April, waiting for robins. Suppose the robins
Chose other woods? There would be only trees.
Brown branches washed in light, sharp against blue,
Brown sodden leaves, and the smell of snow gone under.

                                        1965

THE GREEN OF OATS

There is nothing in this world or any other
Green like the green of young oats bent by the wind
At evening; half an hour maybe to sunset,
When the light is slant. There is no green like that green
Which is silver as well as green, with a little gold in it,
Warm at the root, cool at the wind-licked blade.

No, it's not grass green, fern green, the green cool cave
At the heart of a wave before white water tumbles;
None of those greens. Nothing is green like oats
Bent in the wind, with half an hour to sunset,
But oats.
   God in the blade cries green,
"Say me!" saying itself in the live shimmer.
God in my bones is worshipful and dumb.

1966

MINNESOTA, OCTOBER 30th

If I were a little lighter I could fly
The way brown oak leaves fly this scuttering day,
Over the stubble of corn and the cut hay,
And bone-bare trees against a cobalt sky.
The sun is glorious, but the wind is wry,
And summer's green is a long time blown away.
Grasshoppers buried in leaves hoard one more day
Their little sap before frost sucks them dry.
Wind scours me empty as the round calm eye
Of some old headbone, used and thrown away
In a field corner where piled stones are gray.
If I were a little lighter I could fly.

1966

NARROW FELLOW

Narrow, the ribbon-snake who lives in our basement,
Is slimmer than my finger and maybe as long
As my foot, if he'd stop to be measured. Mostly he's moving,
A green, quick flash, sunlight on wind-licked grass.

Female relatives don't like snakes, even named snakes.
Snakes are for hacking up, not harboring.
Just such Byzantine scales, such a ruby flash
Of tongue came once to a woman in apple shade,
Whispering, "I am food without calories,
Drink without nausea, love with no bed to make after."

Except this shape is older than theology,
Even women who have locked their emptiness
Know it in dreams, the thrust that picks their locks.
Their marrow whispers, "What are pearl and crystal?
Life is a bloody flux."
                              And willow women,
Green women, dancing in a bank-full season,
Every root sweet with sap, remember dryness,
Their tissue mad for water, and no water.

Actual Narrow twists in my warm fingers,
Cool, dry, alive beyond my humanizing.
After he goes, my skin tingles with difference.

1966

DEATH OF THE BIG BUCK

He has taken his last bellyful of our corn,
Fooled his last hunter, fathered his last fawn.
We will not whistle over his prints again,
Cloven, and deep, and big as a man's hand.

There were only the prints before. We never saw him;
Only found his tracks in our corn when the season was over
And said, "Next year." Now there is no more next year.
Some stranger has three hundred pounds of venison

And a perfect rack.
                        His teeth were all worn down.
Nature is not compassionate at harvest;
The hunter's slug was quicker than worms, or starving.
There are other deer, to flash white tails as they bound,

To leave their small sharp prints among our corn rows.
Nothing anymore to bring us down
To our knees, to leave our knuckles gray with dust,
Measuring ourselves by something big and wild.

                                        1968

TEN BELOW

Lake softly luminous under snow.
Slantwise, from the lit house,
The grooves where we pulled out the fish-house
Move into darkness.

Snow over ice
Creaks under my feet. Orion shows faint. High overcast.
I go with the grooves
Into darkness. Beyond is nothing.
Darkness eats me.

Low down, a faint light. Less
Than Orion's foot in the night sky. Low,
Lake level. Light with a hint of gold. Light
Of one candle shining through the rickety boards
Of the second-hand fish house. I grope at the door.

"Anything?"

"A couple."

In small gold warmth I take off my outer mittens.

1973

BIRDWATCHING: FOR TIM

You never can name them all,
Though you walk from sun to sun,
With a field guide in your hip pocket
And field glasses on.
Always some bright new flutterer
Flashes out and is gone
Before your eye takes its color
Your ear gets its song.

You never can name them all,
Though you walk till your feet burn.
Always one more small valley
Opens like a new heaven,
If heaven had prickly ash;
And then there's a different one
Singing a variation;
Then, in a flutter, gone.

You never will get them all
With your finite life list words.
Is it thrush there, or warbler,
Fluting those minor thirds?
You will sink down after walking
Into dark soft as feathers
Dark ending, dark beginning;
Found by your lost birds.

1974

88

PRICKLY ASH

In rural life the prickly ash
Is no damned good to man or beast.
Where sweet wild raspberries hide their cache
It bars the berry-pickers' feast.

Its thorns prick high, its boughs swing low,
It stabs the shiftiest and the quickest;
The very place you want to go,
Is where the prickly ash is thickest.

It gives man neither fruit nor flower;
No crop but what the eye can pick.
Its bright green lemony leaves smell sour;
And Jesus, how its thorns do prick!

Suburban gentlemen in suits
Drive out to measure and survey;
As dust beneath the builder's boots
Is land which does not pay its way.

Flatten her out, boys, get her clear!
Down with vegetable trash!
Man's be the ultimate ecosphere.
....
Sic 'em, sic 'em, prickly ash!

1975

BLACKBIRDS

A patch of sky suddenly detached, descending
In a hail of wings. Brown, off-black, black, iridescent
As they catch the light. Starlings, grackles, blackbirds,

Filling every tree of the grove with their brass-voiced blackguard,
Yelling across the bright cool morning, "Choing, choing,"
Moving always one tree ahead of me, going up

In a rush and roar of wings. (Passenger pigeons
Lived here once. Flocks roared like railroad trains.
They blackened the sun. They are all gone.)

Moving out across the fields now, the dark cheerful louts
Of September, despoiling corn
As if they owned the field, going on again

With that flash and roar of wings, the last of them gone
With the last leaves, the last lisp
Of summer's clothing bright on the ground
Under darkening skies.

1978

MARCH

Wind, then fog, then rain. The first since November.
The kids griping. Ice underfoot.
The white walls along the driveway
Beginning to slump and gray. The gander treading
The white goose in honeycombed, rotten snow.
Everyday now the melt saucers around the trees
Growing a little bigger. All the winter trash
Surfacing as the snow melts.
Today, going out to water the pig
With her litter of ten, I heard some bird
Not part of the winter gang;
Gray feathers on a gray branch, against gray sky.
Any night now the penned geese
Answering the wild ones.

1979

HEARING THE WHITE-THROAT IN OCTOBER

Sudden in bare trees
The fluting of the white-throated sparrow.
That bird of early sun, miraculous leaves,
Crumble of bare earth
As I dropped beans into the furrow.

Today the trees are mostly unleaved,
The grasses ash-colored, the tune
A going-south tune.

The flute of the white-throat wanders and hesitates
As I bury tulip bulbs with cold hands.

1980

WHEN YOUR ANIMALS DIE

When your animals die, they die. There is no technique
Does you any good. You cannot blow
Life through those slimed nostrils, air
Through the mouth with the oats on the teeth
Into the still lungs.
They lie there,

And the Rescue Squad does not come screaming with its machinery
To trick the heart and make the limp legs dance.
For animals
There is no death watch, no Intensive Care.

The hard head that hung up inside
Against the mother's bone,
Till you slipped your hand in and guided it out of there,
Lies like a stone. The meat and bone
You fed and watered, shoveled out after,
Penned up and medicated,
Has escaped your care.
The light in the clever unhuman eyes
Has gone off somewhere.

When animals die there is no valediction,
Beyond the head shake and straightening shoulders,
And, "Shit. Ah, shit!"
Or for some old breeder whose death
Cheated the chance to ship her out,
A last nudge with a manured boot, and a muttered,
"Well, we didn't lose no money on that one."

Neither hymn nor headstone.
Small ones you dig holes for, the big ones

You call the rendering plant, and their truck comes out.
(One of the drivers for Central Bi-Products
Has a sign on the front of his truck that says, "Black Vulture.")
The corpse that frisked and gobbled and bred
Is hoisted in with the limp smelly others,
And hauled away
Where they do what they do with them there.

1984

MAY DAY: TWO-TENTHS OF AN INCH

Hardly any snow all winter,
Hardly any rain all spring.
Leaf-litter crunching, month-old grass
Spiky underfoot.
All the leaves came on in a rush.

Planting beans yesterday, dust
In my nose, in my shoes, dust
In my pores, the ground under the hoe
Like broken brick.
Watching clouds build, wishing
My little legumes well.

Those guys cannot feel this,
In their cloud-topping world-skimming jets;
On the forty-eighth floor, in the soft kiss
Of air-conditioned comforts;
At the summits, behind
The bullet-proof glass.

Not tossing
As the dry wind shakes
These too-early leaves.
Not shooting up straight in bed sniffing for smoke,
In a nightmare of wildfire in dead-dry grass.

No feel of the dust and fear,
No amazed delight
As the small drops plop on the roof,
And we turn in a rush of sweetness, touch while we can.

One ear still tuned
To that small inconstant music.
Let it come, let there be nurture, oh give us kindness
For the heart's affections and the tender shoots.

1984

STORM, EARLY NOVEMBER

Black tatters of zucchini leaf, ash-colored shreds
Of bean pods;
Last lost tomatoes, white and flabby,
And the clumsy bonsai of broccoli
I was picking two weeks back.

The trees roaring, the grey sky tumbled, bits of snow
Whipping my face. The wind
Snatching heat from my body,

Ripping loose the plastic
From the barn window.

As I open the door, one of the six-month lambs
Jumps the feed trough all in one motion;
But they turn and run back and bump each other
Over the poured-out feed.

Grinding of jaws,
And the sun smell of grain.

1984

TURN

The trees shiver,
Summer falls down.
Shudders of gold, red, bronze,
Rain, wind, drunk sun,

Rustle and fall and fade
Into beetlehome, wormworld,
All those mouths and webs
Of the one-cell changers.

And the limbs lift clear,
Gray against blue.
A nakedness of turning
Which ends, turns

To gray lisp, white shimmer,
And the long still cold,
Orion striding darkness
Toward spring stars.

1985

NARROW FELLOW, AGAIN

Reading a poem first published twenty years
after I wrote it

Jesus Christ, I was thirty-one.
Eight years married, only two kids;
Full of lust and theories.

Who was that woman?

But the snake's still here
In these old words,
Green flash and shimmer and long flow
Of strange muscles
In my ignorant hands.

Quicktongue, shapechanger, hello.
Little brother, brother,
Hello.

1986

THE LAND LIFTS CLEAR

Now the land lifts clear
Of its winter covering.
Grimed snow crumpling away
From hilltop and thicket,
Sluicing down gullies, pooling in marshes
Where the red-wings tip and scream,
Where the floating bleach jug
And the pitched-out beer cans flash.

The candid light of April
Makes sharp shadows
Of naked trees, lays its gold
On ash-brown tangles of last year's dead grass.

We too lift in this clear air,
Homo sapiens, most complex of beasts;
Let loose in our souls, like winnowing snipe
Whistling hope over bare fields.
"We can begin again! We can make it all new!"
Drunk on the amazing grace of unmetered sunlight,

As if gravity could relent, as if history
Will melt like the walls of some forsaken farmhouse,
All our old dreams and nightmares drowned in leaves.
Foundation stones square where the barn was,
Spilled hoops marking the silo,
All of it mellowing into earth,

As if the newer walls were not high and strong,
The new silos with their aimed seed
Not always in season;
Laying out trajectories of hate, perpetual winters
Of the terrorized heart.

Still, we come out of our hunched houses,
Lift our eyes to returning birds, go back
To dull fields re-greening, sharp trees
Veiling themselves in the new year,

To our old torn mother, tough and scarred and alive
Under the flight of our dreaming souls.

1988

BAIT

There is bait for every taste,
Doughball, and leech, and worm,
And the glittering artificials
That flash and twist where the sun
Pours down through dust-specked water
To the blood-gilled airless ones;
Yes, you will take the right bait
When the right bait comes.

Hooked in lip or gill cover,
Kicking in strangling air,
Whistled and shouted over and dropped
Into the live well.
Then the mystical transformation,
To the china and napery,
After the species with shining knives
Cuts all the waste away.

Or, ripping the bloody barb out
And twisting back on down,
Till fungus and gas in the tissues
Lifts them to rise again,
To the sullen beak of the snapper
Or the raccoon's washed hands,
Or the long-legged heron lifting away
On her great slow wings.

1990s

NORWEGIAN (OR BROWN) RAT

Written for inclusion in John Caddy's "Morning Earth" website, accompanied by an illustration of the subject of his invitation Invite to Write #70

Startled, attacking, *rattus norviegicus*
Leaps at the camera, shows every tooth in his jaws.
Thrusts out defensively his deft little paws;
A widely-distributed mammal. Rather like us.
Our little brown stowaway, thriving on our leavings.
Tamed, he's the scientist's friend. He runs those mazes.
Makes our drugs safer. Dies of our diseases.
Wild, he's a forager, just out to make a living.
Has no respect for property. Pays no tax.
Breeds well, and often. Partial to mac and cheese,
But gets along fine on foods less appealing than these.
Romps with his friends in cheerful ratty packs.
He thrives on what we squander. He grows fat!
We find that disgusting. So we hate the rat.

2014

THREE THINGS I LEARNED IN MY EIGHTIETH YEAR

In my eightieth year I discover with great pleasure
That I can decrypt a few silver lyrics
From the musical chaos of the June world.
After long trying, now I can disentangle
Wren, robin, oriole, indigo bunting,
Rose-breasted grosbeak.

How good is all new knowledge!
How lovely the world, always
More many-voiced than we knew.

Maybe in fifteen more I can learn the warblers,
If I am present, if I still can listen.

2016

IT MAKES NO DIFFERENCE TO THE WREN

The leaves show their back sides, all pale,
As the branches prostrate themselves;
As the whole tree thrashes, resists, bends more,
Screams its cry of broken wood and gives up
Part of itself,
And the rain slams down like bullets.

The house wren sings through it all.
A small melodious persistent warble,
Sweet to human ears,
But with a little hiss in it,
And amazing volume for so small a bird.

Because, to the wren, it makes no difference
If the sky suddenly fires its wild artillery,
And a sword of light singes the eyes,
Slamming into some part of the world
Which is not the wren's nest.
No mate of his inside, no eggs
Sprung from his cloacal kiss,
No naked fledglings opening huge beaks
For the succulent parental bug.

His little fortress is, for the moment, safe,
But his song never alters,
Because, for the wren, it is all, always
Danger! Danger! Danger!
The poison in the bug, the beak
Of the blue jay,
(Feeding his own, as the wren feeds his own),
Even the beak of another wren, another male
Hungry for nest space and mating.

It is all peril and catastrophe, one
Nesting after another,
But the small song is still sweet, sweet.

And this storm is past. Plants reach roots
For the new water.
Broken boughs settle toward leaf-mold and compost,
Death accepted, a permanent part of the composition,
Which is always, also, decomposition.
The wren sings, sings Danger!
But also Joy!
For this mate, this brood, his small protective warning.
Season to season,
It makes no difference to the wren.

2017

YOUNG HAWKS

One summer, two young Sharp-Shinned Hawks
Landed close to the bird feeders.
Their parents are fast little predators, deft flyers
Between the branches of our woods. As the guide says,
They "take birds to the size of pigeons."

But these young ones
Could not stick the landing.
Came down bouncing, breaking twigs,
Squawking indignantly, not where they planned to be.

Jays hollered, crows cawed, every songbird was gone!
Except of course the chickadees,
Who gave these unwelcome guests an extra warning "dee dee,"
Then went on whipping in and out
With seeds in their beaks.

And the hummingbirds, those little flying needles
Had no fear, as they have no fear of anything.
Being too small, too fast, not even a mouthful.
The house wrens, too, just hunkered down
In their brush tangles, to scold, and scold, and scold!

Three or four days those young hawks hung around,
Flapping from branch to branch,
Like boys in the interim between childhood's nimbleness
And the earned stride of manhood, at the stage
Where feet catch and trip and elbows send dishes flying.

By day three or four the feeders
Were busy again.
Nuthatches, grosbeaks, finches, even the male oriole,

All gold and black and glorious,
Teaching his almost as glorious young
The wonders of grape jelly.

And the hawks were not to be seen or heard.
Maybe gone to somebody else's feeder.
Or perhaps, having learned the ways of their wings,
They had become what they were meant to be:
Deft flyers, part of the natural woodland assembly,
Beautiful small birds, beautiful and lethal.

2017

4

Bare-Voiced Song

TO CERTAIN PROFESSORS

Show us how he did it. Show us how ingeniously the labials and dentals
Are arranged to produce the proper effects. Show us how the placement
Of a preposition in line two is intimately related
To the Adonis myth, via Eliot; the general structure
Is of course Elizabethan, despite the fact
That he sat at the feet of Father Hopkins,
Though reluctantly, and, as it were,
With his bags packed.

Maybe hung over, harassed by phones and neighbors;
Noting his lapdog's limp, hearing Death clear
His throat in the laundry-box among the clothes,
When the wild horse neighed and battered down the wall.

His seat was wrong, and the reins broke off in his hands,
And his skull split with the bucking curveting prance,
But he held till the mad sky fell, he rode, he rode
Down slopes of apocalypse in desperate dance.

1955

SONG FOR MASTER YEATS

I walked up through the spring abundance of woods
To the hilltop field, alfalfa to my knees,
Through the luminous green of gooseberry and fern,
The six-weeks-out-of-snow prodigal fleece of the trees.

Finding the sparrow's nest on the ground again.
Stalking the rose-breasted grosbeak by his song.
Over the paling sky night-hawks and swallows
Danced for their supper with ravenous feather and tongue.

Every branch of a tree in the woods had singing fruit;
A loon cried, out on the lake. The night-hawks kept flying.
I watched till spots of black came in my eyes,
And stumbled home on legs I could not feel.

Yeats prayed to sing out of a golden throat,
Unchanging bird in changeless Byzantium.
Though I have sent my passions to the furnace,
I'd pray to sing, if I could be reborn,

On a perilous twig, to shiver with early frost,
Love between thistles, lay between gray stones,
Sweep May skies, wheel in May air my season,
With a hard mouth and hollow, singing bones.

1965

IN MEMORIAM: PABLO NERUDA

As the old poet dies, the soldiers
Ransack houses, including his.
With arms full of books, magazines, newspapers, they clatter
Down stairs and across gray sidewalk to dump their load.

The colonel has two chins. The warm face
Of a *paterfamilias* leans to the microphone,
Smiles for the lens of the Yankee journalist.
"But these are bad books, senor. We burn only bad books."

The small flare flickers, catches, eats
At the edge of the page. The soldiers dump, and run
Up the stairs, glance or do not glance
At titles, some in languages foreign to them.
Lenin, *Playboy*, Truman Capote,
Chairman Mao, sheaves of anonymous manuscript
Feed the growing bonfires.

"Of course I would know a good book, senor."
(Leaning close to the microphone, the smooth large smiling face.)
"A good book is a book from which I can learn something,
Or a book which will help me to teach another person."

As the orange-red eats up the print, the black margin
Runs before, the calcined words
Visible for a second before they crumble.
Half a page, a quarter page, nothing.

The sport stadium is full of detainees,
And one sometimes hears distant gunfire,

But there is no public disorder. The two-chinned colonel
Is through being interviewed, returns to his work.

And the bonfires blaze up, here, here, here,
Down the long gray street, making circles of warmth, lifting
Occasional charred leaves on the wind of burning,
Which float, sometimes, remarkable distances.

1973

SEBASTIAN MELMOTH CLIMAXES HIS ACT
BY SMASHING HIS GUITAR
For Dan, Jethro Tull, and Queen

Stoned on the smoky sun of five p.m.,
I think of thick-fingered lads less lucky than me;
Finishing shifts where the tankers' engines thrum,
Rocked to the bitter beat of the North Sea.
Some folks have sung bare-voiced and picked unamplified;
(I practice while the roadies check my sets.)
Some voices have stormed heaven before they died;
But then they died, and never made the charts.

Think now, I say to the mammal in my mirror;
Millions of years of dinosaurs and ferns,
Ground, crushed, grown hot, the world's most vintage liquor,
Sweated out, sold, in lamp and streetlight burns.
Me and my lads, turned out, turned on, and turning
Our slickest tricks, with sequins on our butts,
Play my new song, "Go Suck It," bravely burning
In light to light a thousand colliers' huts.

Oh the sharp-breasted screaming snack-bar lasses,
Oh the thick-fingered lads with motorbikes
And pocky skin behind their smoky glasses,
Hang on our gestures, scream when we toss our mikes.
Here's old Sebastian, burning in his socket,
(Oh give us power and light) till the filaments fry;
Blazing down heaven like a bloody rocket.
(I'll bust their fucking charts before I die.)

"Do it!" they scream. I make my newest faces.
(Blank faces light. They have seen, they have touched a star.)
One blues, three rockers, splits, now bugger the bassist,

Spit fire, and bust my second-best guitar.
After the tricks they leave. Sometimes we jam,
Or talk, or screw, or score, or just get sick;
In the cool, stony light of five a.m.,
After I play the music, I play the music.

I think of dark rooms where thick-fingered lads
Splash water on their heads and break their hearts.
I sing one bare-voiced song, and go to bed.
(They are stone dead, and never made the charts.)

1978

THEY'VE PACKED UP THE ROCK AND ROLL

They've packed up and gone away with the rock and roll
Records I bought them for Christmas, but played on my own.
They've left shelves full of dust mice behind; and now their old lady
Will have to go tell the world to shove it alone.

No more of those screaming guitars and screaming tires,
Drum-busting drummers, and sagas of busted friends.
Now I can mellow listening to temperate claviers,
Sanctified organs, respectable violins.

No tenors to snarl along with me when I holler;
No back-beat to lend percussion to my rages.
I can grow some habits to match my twenty white hairs;
Grow into my age, before I belong to the ages.

They've packed up the jacket-lyrics and left me to hear
The news, and the beat of my heart, and rain over stones.
To sing in my half-empty house, of my half-done life,
To pick it off on my own mean old bones.

1981

FLOWING WATER
In Memoriam: Edith Eleanor Rigsby Alcock

The visiting artist calls, "Who did the painting over the stairs?"
Clouds, mountains, a house, trees;
The shape of a woman, done with a stroke or two,
Maybe washing clothes (the canvas is dim)
By flowing water.

That painting was in my house as long as I can remember.
Dad said, "Your grandmother painted that
When she was a young woman."

The woman I was named for,
Around as long as I can remember.
Born in the 1870's, fought
For the right to take nurse's training.
Married, at thirty, a patient
Much older than she was.
Hard times. Widowhood. Long years
In her youngest son's house.

"This is really not bad." The visiting artist
Is in his twenties. "I like the way
She makes this light on the water.
Who did she study with?"

A question I never asked; she was Grandma,
Who once looked in the mirror,
Lifted plump old arms, and said to the reflection,
"Where's Edie, where's she gone?"

The visiting artist almost touches the brush strokes
Which make light on flowing water.
Marks of hands
Buried in '45.

1983

WRITING LATE

Switch off the typewriter,
Push back the chair.
I had not known my back
Was so stiff, my feet so cold.
Brain arcing and spitting,
But the chapter is over.

Turn off lights, walk in dark
Into the bedroom. Numb feet
Scrape out of shoes, body
Sheds the day.
The slow rhythm of John's breath
Makes in the dark an island

To which I swim through cold sheets, blue fire
Still sparking behind my eyes.
Body at ease, mind
Afloat between stars. Skin to skin.
Falling asleep, I feel my toes.

1983

THE POETRY OF SOMALIA

"Poetry is important in Somalia and deals with such subjects as war, peace, women, horses, and camels."—Entry, "Somalia," *Encyclopedia Britannica*, 15th edition, Vol. II
In Memoriam: Claire van Breeman Downes, 1926-2013

Under the high summer sky of the American Midwest,
A Somali woman is working in the community garden
Next to the Unitarian Fellowship. She wears billowing Biblical robes,
No part of her visible but her dark face and hands.

How strange we must have looked to her
When she was new to this country, this town;
American women, bare-armed, bare-legged,
Greeting male friends with hugs, going together
Into their odd sanctuary without muezzin or cross,
To remember a friend who has died.
Though we grieve, no one will wail.
We are, as we say in these parts,
Celebrating the life of Claire Downes.

No talk of God or heaven, only
Our voices singing together,
And her husband, her children, two grandsons reading her poems:
Books, college, falling in love, the stuff of her life.
Five kids. All those moves. Later the teaching.
Always the laundry, the kids, the housework, the bills,
The stacks of student papers, the red pen.
Always a face or bottom to wipe,
Always an argument to settle, always tears to assuage,

Always poetry like a gathering anvil
Of cloud on the horizon,

The distant flash, the growing rumble, the sometime moment snatched,
In which she could rush out, oh glory, and be drenched.

When we come away from the stained glass
And the air conditioning, that other woman
Is still in the garden, laboring in the heat
Down rows of future dinners.
She does the work of Eve, head down, bent forward
From the waist,
Dark fingers stirring dark earth, making things grow.

Now, as we say goodbye to each other, clasping our books of poems,
The gardener swings back up, pressing
Her hands to the small of her back,
Easing tired muscles.
Who will write the poem of her life?

Now she calls out in her African tongue
To the boy in shorts and tee shirt and sneakers,
Maybe six or eight, who is playing
In the green field beyond the garden.
He answers absently, as children will
While they are living out
The great poem of being young.
And she bends again to her work,
While he runs, runs,
And his bare knees flash in the sun.

2013

OLD MAN ON A SOUTHERN ROAD
Remembering the Swingin' Deacon

"Quite natty," my son says,
About the elderly black man walking
In suit and street shoes
Down the shoulder of Highway 80
On the outskirts of Savannah, Georgia,
On a day of rare snow.

Son and wife got him in to warm up—
It was freezing out there.
Persuaded him to accept first coffee, then hot soup.

His name was, he said, Benton Williams;
And he was bound for Statesboro, fifty miles west,
But maybe it was the used car auction,
A mile down the road, to
Pick him up a hundred dollar car.

Eventually he agreed maybe
A lift to the Union Gospel Mission
(That refuge for the homeless and confused)
Was not a bad idea.

Eric says he talked a lot in the car,
Hard to understand, except when he said,
"I used to be in radio, on the Negro stations."

The old man got off at the mission,
And hearing Eric's story brought back to me
The velvet voice of the Swingin' Deacon,
"Spinning the latest and greatest rhythm and blues"
On an Oakland station,

How voice and music poured
Into our living room
On the white side of the bay,
My sister and I turning the family radio
High, dancing to "Blueberry Hill,"
"Work With Me, Annie," B.B. (the Blues Boy) King,
And a young Ray Charles "Doin' the Mess Around."
The Swingin' Deacon held it all together,
The hits, the ads for "Nadanola Bleaching Cream
For lighter, brighter skin," and poetry, maybe his:

"In the cool of the day she walks
Between tall flowers down to a still pool
Where the last light fades—"

And when you are seventeen, finding the music
Which delights you and exasperates your parents,
You do not imagine the hands which lay the needle
Into the black groove. You do not wonder much
How it is when the Deacon goes off shift, and is
Simply another black man on the streets
Of Oakland, California, in 1952.

I hope the girl in his poem was real, and liked poetry;
I hope whatever work he did to earn his bread
He was somehow still, inside, the Swingin' Deacon;
That smooth, that knowing guide to the cool grooves,
And that there was righteous music at his funeral.

And as for Benton Williams down in Georgia,
Old man on a southern road, with his own history,
I hope his memories, real or imagined, were grand,
And wherever he wants to get to, may he get there,
And may he be remembered after he leaves us.

2018

5

Writing In Snow

WILD SEED
For Jim: 1969

Dandelion, wild rose, foxtails: where man begins.
Later, he gets the seeds with germination dates,
Clods rake to rough brown velvet, clean cultivation,
Ranked roots, bug-dusted foliage, predictable parsnips.

Only tough weeds seed in the wild ditches.
Consistent plowmen plow their ditches clean,
Then starve when sudden plagues afflict their parsnips.
They prowl bare ditches mad for something green.

(All this a way to talk with a certain toughness
Of a certain tenderness; neither seed nor son,
But wild hair and grave eyes and roving bones
Gone down the wind in a ditch-plowing time.)

Then sweet bed for your seed, young wanderer,
("Six weeks till frost," whispers the summer grass.)
And fine rain down for every root's dark hunger;
And may the plowmen miss you when they pass.

1969

WRITING IN SNOW

For My Children: December 1980

It all goes on as it has;
Outside the border of Poland
The Russians are on maneuvers; nuns
Come out of their Latin graves.
Outside the student center in letters ten feet high
Someone has tramped out "Lennon" in the snow.

The candles blow out in the wind.
The harmonies blur. The crumpled manifestos
Whip back and forth. It all goes on.
Go home, get bombed, rage
At the human race, go to sleep

Crying while the needle grinds out
"We're Sergeant Pepper's one-and-only Lonely Heart's Club Band."
The snow-writing spreads, blurs,
Giant footprints, a sloppy Rorschach;
The dirty water of mourning washes

By little and little the hard stone.
It all goes on. The voice grows hoarse
Arguing, the fingers type
Till they hurt. The whisper of water
Grinds, grain by grain,

And it takes forever, takes
Brains, hope, courage, heart's blood
To grind down an inch, a yard;
And if the stone splits and the prisoners
Lurch out blinking, some will blench

From the diamond-dazzle of wall-less space, cry,
"It's falling apart, it's all
Falling—" and spend their last strength
Mortaring it back with their own blood.
It all goes on, music

Out of shouts and tears, justice
Out of mobs and old stones, strawberry fields
Out of the loam which was old stone once,
Out of grinding down. It all goes on.

1980

ANN'S RHUBARB
Read at the Funeral of a Peace Worker
In Memoriam: Ann Graves—1894-1985

We knew it was spring when the rhubarb came up at Ann's place,
When we laughed and ate rhubarb cake in the warm air;
The fruit of the earth, and a peaceable couple's dreaming:
Let there be rhubarb picnics everywhere!

Open the gates and the files, let out the rebels,
Give the revolutionaries pantry keys.
Invite the generals to loosen their uniforms
And sit on the warm earth under the flowering trees.

Let economists model and muddle over their beer,
Let the patriots defend their honor at Frisby;
Let the dancers dance the hopak and the high life,
Let the singers sing "Guantanamera" and "Old Kentucky,"

Let the whole world come and eat spring rhubarb at Ann's place,
Sit on warm ground, in a peaceable kingdom come;
At this point in the reading all of us look embarrassed,
At hearing our dreams, so simple, so sweet, so dumb.

It is easier to split atoms than share with strangers,
More glorious to raise banners than green leaves,
Easier to blow up the world than to come together,
To sit on the same ground under the same trees,

Like illiterate beasts who have neither gods nor borders,
Like kids for whom life is food and games and sleep.
To root like dumb plants the inarticulate humus,
With sun to feed us, with only rain to weep.

1985

HIROSHIMA: FOR THE SURVIVORS
August 1985

It must have been a night
Like last night, warm;
Wind cooling damp flesh
Where it touched other flesh—

Though they slept on futons,
Restless with more than heat;
Their men
All gone off to war.

What was to come unimagined
Even by the bombers.
Captain Lewis as the Enola Gay
Rocked with shock waves,

"My God,
What have we done?"
Done. The fried and flayed dead
Beyond excuse or apology,

And the survivors, old
With their bomb-sown diseases,
A few old men and women,
Croaking, "Never again!"

Like the gassed vets of Ypres.
Like starved peasants
In the Hundred Years' War.
Like Priam's daughters,

Gang-raped, dragged
To the Greek ships;
All those eons of crying,
"Never again, never again!"

The human mind forgets, or disallows
What is beyond bearing,
(Though they bore it.)
The human spirit

Is frail as a paper crane,
Whose wings cannot bear us
Out of ourselves;
Easiest to hope and sleep.

While in heaven the satellites
Circle and track, droning
"Reality is an acceptable
Level of casualties."

Reality kills first,
Hoping to survive, but knowing
Freedom is beyond price.
Knowing the patriot heart
Burns to burn, cries,
"Death before dishonor!"

Scattered voices singing
From land to land
In despite
Of all known history,

Singing, "Greatness
Is not brute force
And the one-cadenced millions,
Greatness is our Mother turning

Her blue-green body
In and out of dark,
Countries a sweet blur,
Ripples of mountain, snatches of plain.

Men and women coming home
From work, shutting the door,
Private and safe. Children
Running in sticky-faced, hollering

And getting washed.
The kettle boiling, the oil frying,
Smells of routine love rising
Like a flight of cranes.

1985

BLACK-DIRT COUNTRY
November, 1985

Black-dirt country;
Clods in fall-plowed fields
Catching last glints of light.

Every little town with its white-steepled immigrant church,
Its implement dealer, its store for sale,
Its grain elevator,
The highest point in miles.

The elevator full, the bins full, corn still coming in;
Truck after truck
Out of that black dirt
Which was big bluestem and buffalo and prairie slough
And bones of Sioux and settler—
Coming in. No place to put it,

Every little town with its corn
Poured on the bare ground,
Golden mountains of sun and dust
Scarfed with first snow.

Somewhere way off,
Kids with faces like very old men
Scour the feeding-station cans
With skeleton fingers,
Scraping up the last pinch of mush.

While the back pages of country weeklies
Fill with fine print,
Under the little drawings of tractors and hammers:
"For sale at public auction, 300 acres good tillable land plus house, barn,
outbuildings, equipment and livestock...."

In neat frame houses, women knit
Watching game shows.
Hands stop now and then,
And they look past the screen.

Downtown, hard-fingered men
Hunch over a brew.
They have eaten plenty of dirt in their time.
They are getting ready
To eat it again.

1985

NINETY SECONDS ON LOCAL NEWS

After they show the spy satellite pictures
Of the Chernobyl nuclear power plant,
("It is unclear at this time whether a second meltdown has occurred."),
After the talk about politics, after the medical experts,
After the pictures of grain traders jumping and screaming
And running up wheat futures,
They bring on an old Ukrainian émigré.

In his head the Dnieper
Runs dark and wet, with fish in it.
Women laugh in Ukrainian.
Kids run in the streets of Kiev.
May sun warms the young wheat.

Pain crawls his stubbled face;
He forgets the camera.

"Such a beautiful city, so much history;
Such a beautiful people."

1986

NOW TRENDING

Facebook postings 03/09/2014:
    Sue and Judy celebrate their marriage
    Mike posts a photo of himself when young; 35 comments,
        mostly humorous
    Son Dan is tagged in a photo, talking with an old friend
    Ted posts a movie review
    Grand-daughter Brooke posts pix of cars and cars
    Steve posts a link to a newly-published poem
    Doug posts his usual sermon from the Little Church of the
        Pines, chickadees switching to spring song
    Brooke posts more pix of cars

    Brent blasts greedy movie producers
    Mim posts a meme, old women dancing with abandon
    Chip, in Thailand, thanks friends who helped him get a new
        bike when the old one was smashed, reports he's
        healing nicely
    Mark, in Malaysia, talks theater
    Tom posts a photo of vineterta, an Icelandic pastry much
        esteemed by our mutual friend Bill, now dead of a
        heart attack,
    after those last poems still raging out fine things.

    Isaac, in Cairo, mourns the recent death of his friend
        Ali Mustafa,
    Photographer and activist, killed in Syria
    By a barrel bomb.
    Later postings by news services confirm this report.

Trending tonight: persistent love, defiant marriage,
Youth, friendship, art,

Escape, adventure, joy, spring,
Vineterta, death, good memory.
Death.

Death.

2014

GONE
Remembering Jacob Wetterling

The helicopter hovers over the place
Where the bones were found.
Twenty-seven years since the man snatched the boy
From the side of the country road,
Telling the brother and his friend to run.
All these years the bones
Were buried in this place
Twenty miles from the boy's home.

The helicopter hovers
Over pasture and clustered trees.
After this rain-rich summer
The trees are densely green.
Cows walk in the meadow, Holsteins
Easy at their grazing.
Pickups buzz by on the two-lane road.

The reporter underlines these details.
Nobody knew, all these years;
Nobody noticed anything strange.

There was only decay,
And the unconcerned cows, the farmer on his tractor,
The passerby on the road, and the people in their houses
Living their lives,

Even as their televisions would have shown the face, over and over,
Of the lost boy,
Of his mother, every year remembering, asking,
"Where is my son?"
And the helpful annual sketch

Altered as if to show age,
As boy became man,
As these bones have never done.

The man who knew, the man who led the police here,
Who stood in court and explained how the boy was taken,
What the boy said, how the boy was touched, when the boy cried
(Which it took a long time for him to do)—
That man knew, all these years,
While the rest of us lit candles, prayed, left yard lights on.

That man's face in the booking picture
Is simply an aging face,
Broad, bearded, plain,
A face like many we have known.

It does not tell us how a man
Comes down to hiding bones.

Surely for the killer—yes, for him, too,
There would be the sound of leaves
In light wind, and the warm smells
Of summer's end and the coming of fall.
For him, too, the slow animal pleasure
Of cows grazing,
And the homecoming after labor, the day's end meal,
The easy chat in the company of others.

For him these things, these ordinary joys
Which are more than enough for us,
Must have been as nothing.
There must have been some incomprehensible need
To grab, to compel, to destroy.

There must have been some terrible joy
In doing what he did.
But the face of the terrible man
We have looked for all these years
Is like any other face.
There is no crazed leer. There is no mark of the beast.

Now they will bring the lost boy home
And the church will be full, and the funeral enormous,
And those who hoped for so long
Will get on with what's left of their lives.
Now at least they know. Their boy is gone,
But his bones are home.

Once there must have been another boy,
An innocent, or the spark of one,
Inside the terrible man
With the ordinary face.

Nobody knows when that boy left,
Or where that boy has gone.

2016

THE JOY OF COOKING

The horrible world pours into my breakfast kitchen
As I take down The Joy of Cooking.

>Says the factual Saturday voice on the radio,
>This morning other people not unlike me
>Are killing and being killed
>In Ukraine, in a city whose name will be forgotten;
>Also in Syria, Libya, North Africa.
>Last week there were other places. Next week, who knows?

I lift down canisters and sifter, get out mixing bowls,
Begin to measure.

>Children are stolen, the girls
>Used for sex, the boys
>Turned into soldiers.
>Others of the young
>Come willingly at the call of a vengeful God,
>Pick up the weapons, strap the explosives on.

I take out buttermilk, I take out eggs, put bacon on.
Its scent and sizzle bless
A small house where two old people
Have loved each other long.

I crack the egg with care, remember my mother
Teaching me this small domestic magic,
The golden yolk and the white each neatly
Dropping into its separate bowl.
The eggbeater which I have owned God knows how long
Sings its rattling song and turns clear liquid

Into a little flying skirt of froth;
Billows of lightness to leaven up the dough.

    Lightness and grace and loving long
    Are little esteemed out there, where they send out the videos,
    Here a beheading, there an immolation.

My son down in Georgia has three hens in his yard;
His children run out to find eggs, have that delight
Of the warm ovoid clutched in the proud small hand.
I am glad they can know that joy, though what good it will do them
Is something the horrible world cannot imagine.

    The killing goes on, despite
    Attempts at mediation,
    Says the radio, bringing me voices
    Of courageous people who want me to know, to remember
    The name of that town, the sounds of that shelling,
    The cries. The cries of those children.
    Remember, and get the facts straight!

Then (for this is Saturday morning),
A little jazz, an account of a family reunion,
And sports, and an old blues man, and a book review.

As if to say, our species is capable of falling in love
With the world in its beautiful particularity,
And ordinary human beings in theirs.

And this, too, is news, or should be.
So I have to believe as I drop the batter on.

                             2015-2017

6

Damned Fine Drumming

PILLAR OF GOLD

The ash tree on the other side
Of our finished garden
Is a pillar of gold this morning.

Leaves pour off in a steady stream down the wind,
Summer's gold flying, season's end.

Yesterday I dug onions, carrots, beets;
Today I ache in every bone
As I hang out laundry; but I can do it.
It needs to be done. Rain is likely tomorrow.
I hang out, we hang on here
In the house we built, as long as we can,
Though at times it seems our golden days are gone.

By late afternoon, I cut the tops
Of yesterday's roots, and store them in sand.
Sturdy provender
For the cold days to come.

And the ash tree is no longer gold,
Save for a few leafy remainders.
Its summer is spent, scattered in gardens and woods.
It stands in October sun, down to its bones.

It will, as they all do, rot
In due time, be felled or fell itself,
Crumble down into soil for future seasons.

The way of the tree is a good way.
But for now, I carry inside
What we grew this year, and store it away.

October 1, 2013

LEAN IN

It is good to lean into the work,
Pushing the body to its limits
And a little beyond,
Though "beyond" is nearer now
Than it was when we began,

And I must remember water, my garden hat,
Sensible shoes, sunscreen, bug repellent,
Not just throw myself at the work
As I did when I was young
And citified and soft,
And thought any pain might be lethal.

Now I know lethal;
My friends die of it.

And throwing myself at the work
Was how I learned;
Failing as much as I succeeded,
But succeeding enough.

My husband grumbles at how little
We do in a day;
"I can't get nearly as much done
As I did twenty years ago."
I point out that twenty years ago he was sixty-six.
Very few jobs too big for us then!

So, lean into the work, push,
Though rising from my knees
I have to come up butt-first, like a cow,
(With always the apt phrase "butt-first like a cow"

Echoing in my head),
Feeling fully my age, the world rocking a little
Before it settles
Into June green and weedy equilibrium,
And the cardinal belting out, "What cheer! Cheer! Cheer!"

I look back on my half-done row
And, for this much, I'm glad,

And for the rest, this is soft dirt:
(He ran the tiller this morning).
One could fall worse places than here.

2015

RIVER

Under our still-bright days and still-good nights
Runs a slow, continuous river of loss.
Rilling along, an andante of goodbyes,
Mostly unnoticed, unheeded, unseen,
Save for the sudden freshet that tears what's dear away.

Often enough we're glad for that river, it does good work.
Who needs that old trash of memory
After all this time, who cares
Just what bad words were said to whom, by whom,
About what lost affection or endeavor
Sixty plus years ago? Let the dark river take it!

And the water, that in the end takes all,
Let it soothe the torn place
Where some chunk of yourself
Failed, and was gone
Before you knew it was gone.

Once, we fished that river,
Easily afloat; cast our bait, pulled in
Those small bright other lives. We tore them from their element,
Ate their tender flesh, consigned their bones
To the current that took them downstream.

We swam that river, washing away
The slime of life, the bright scales
Of those lives we had eaten.

We sat at ease on the banks of that river,
Watching the broken glitter of our small reflected fire,

Then lay down by that water.
It sang easily through our dreaming all night long.

Whatever we have lost to it, what lives,
Loves, ambitions, abilities,
The silt of it feeds other lives downstream.

There are worse ways to go
Than this slow washing away.
And anyway, the river gives no choice.

2015

TIGER

In the last scraps of sleep
After a night of broken rest,
I dream myself a Tiger.

In my own corporeal being
I am a sick old lady
Who slept, but mostly didn't,
In a borrowed bed far from home,

But Tiger, Tiger is strong.
Tiger is gold and black and young,
And is, when it pleases him, Mr. Tiger.
Mr. Tiger wears a dashing scarf, a porkpie hat,
And very cool shades,
Mr. Tiger plays piano
In the bars of New Orleans.

Even as I cough myself awake,
Even as my husband says, "You sound awful,"
(And I do!)

Tiger is strong in me. Between coughs
I tell my husband the dream.
He says, "Where do the ears go, with that porkpie hat,
Over or under?"
And I can't remember, but I assume
That Tiger's ears, like all the rest of Tiger,
Go just anywhere Mr. Tiger wants to go.

> "Don't tell me you feel fine," my husband is saying,
> "I think you need to be in the hospital,
> Under an oxygen tent."

I tell him a few more days and we'll be home,
And I don't think they use oxygen tents anymore.

Tiger goes just where Tiger wants to go.
Down at the yacht club the millionaires cry, "Tigah!
Haven't seen you, old man. How's for a drink?
Tell us your recent adventures! And then some billiards—"

I have been coughing, coughing all night long,
Every cough bringing a flinch from him.

Tiger, of course, is greeted with tears of joy
At the day-care.
Brave little toddlers scramble up on his back,
Feeling the mighty bones
And the sleek and sinuous stride.
Very good children get to lie on his belly
Snuggled in soft fur, feeling him breathe, taking in
The mighty beat of his heart
And the rumble of his purr.

Poor man, he's had maybe less sleep than me,
All night long helping
With Kleenex, cough drops, cough syrup, gobs of honey,
None of which worked for long.

When Mr. Tiger strides into a low den
Things slowly fall silent till the old barkeep
Says, "Lordy, who's that?
Why, I do believe it is Mr. Stripes himself!"

Even as my husband rains down suggestions for health
Which sound more and more like orders,
I know this man loves me.

We are not young tigers anymore,
Not so swift, not so tough, not so strong,
And he does not want to lose me,
Nor I him.

Does Mr. Tiger have anything like these worries?
Maybe after the last of the drinkers go home,
When the chairs are going up on the tables,
Hat and scarf and shades laid aside,
In an empty room, in the dark end of the night,
Claws stretch into old, time-twisted fingers,
And Mr. Tiger plays a final song.
Mean and low down, he remembers, he remembers,
He lays all out (remembers, he remembers),
A last performance of "The Empty Bed Blues."

2016

AS I AM DYING

As I am dying, I hope I can be looking
Into the tops of trees.
(I could show you the trees.)
Nor will it matter greatly
If they are just putting out tiny frail leaves,
Or if they are billowing with summer.
Of if it's fall, fall, and the reds, the bronzes, the golds!
Or if every shred of leaf
Has fallen away, and my trees
Are bare as bones, against hard winter sky.

That is what I want, but none of it will matter.
I should not write these words
Which my children may read, and, loving me,
Try to make happen, and find that difficult.

Who knows what the dead see?
The trees they will one day compost,
Or strange walls, medicine's machinery,
Or faces briefly known.

I think of our old friend who is making that journey.
Sometimes he knows us, though not what year it is;
Will turn from what we say, to respond
To other persons in the room, whom he sees,
Though we cannot.

Sometimes he holds a full conversation,
His questions being answered. He laughs
At jokes made by the long dead, who seem to laugh back.

At the end, perhaps we reach out
To what we have loved,
Though it has long since gone to mulch and memory.

In time we are all like those people in his room,
A compost of lived life,
A tremor in the air, like the fall of leaves.

2016

JIM, SLIDING

At this morning's visit, Jim is time-sliding.
As soon as we come into his room,
He tells us, "I've found Dee!
She's working in St. Cloud!"

And we do not question or argue,
Though Dee, his wife, whom we also loved,
Has been dead ten years.

His talk slides from past to present to past,
As waves slide into waves.
"An important development in medicine occurred yesterday."
The names come from fifty or sixty years back,
And he knew those men, so it's all likely true,
Though his "yesterday" happened during his visitors' childhood,
And those colleagues are no longer in practice.

In other visits, he's not sure who we are,
And sometimes he talks to those not present.
My husband once sat by his side, unacknowledged,
In a conversation during a long-ago baseball game.
Jim asks questions, waits for answers
Which sound only in his mind.
"When's the next practice?
I think it's about time we went for some beer!"

If we could fix him in this place and time
He still could not leave this room.
He would not stride confidently in his white coat
To see patients, confer with colleagues,
Make diagnoses and decisions.
With or without his wife, he won't again welcome us
To the house he loves.

We won't sit on the deck looking out over the lake,
He won't drink beer with us, talk politics, tell old stories.

And now he has slid into his late teens.
The time the blizzard blocked traffic on the roads,
Blocked the train which brought medicine
To his father's pharmacy, for the four hundred people
In that town, and its outlying farms.

"Insulin had to be refrigerated back then," he tells us,
"We'd get it from Sauk and people would pick it up,
But now we were out, and Dad knew that in a couple of days,
Without their injections, people would start to die."

This is a story he loves to tell,
And now he is in that story, on cross-country skis
With his pal Roger, skimming the miles
Over snowy drifts.
Two strapping small-town boys, knowing
They were doing something hard and necessary
But important too, kidding each other, waving
To snow-bound farmers shoveling toward their barns.
Loading up in Sauk Centre, maybe grabbing coffee and pie,
Then turning around and heading home.

Here he is, young and strong, moving stride for stride
With his best friend.
Everything ahead of him, the University,
The long study learning a loved art,
The white coat, the marriage, the children,
The jobs, the triumph, the life.

Here they come, skimming the drifts of those long miles,
With rescue in their knapsacks, sliding home.

2013-2017

DAMNED FINE DRUMMING

I dreamed we were at one of those gatherings
We went to, back then.
Somebody's rented farmhouse with salvaged furniture,
Bright small wall hangings from central America.
Blue jeans, tie die, brown rice,
Smells of wood smoke and night outdoors.

Drank home brew, talked organic farming,
Composting outhouses, self-reliance, solidarity,
Alternatives. Alternatives!

The good old music was new, then,
And we never the youngest, but oh God, young;
And some of us in that dream, as I realized later,
Gone on the long trip out now, gone.

Then I was naked, wrapped in a sheet.
Somebody said, in a voice of imminent fun,
"Are you ready for burial, Edith?" And I said, "Sure."
But then I remembered, and said,
"Oh, if it's a sauna, I can't.
I got a pacemaker three weeks ago,
So I can't."

And that was okay.
The party was still going on, just the crowd thinner,
When the sound began.
     Brmm brmm brmm brmm
Drums, drums, they were drumming
In the next room.
     Crazy Horse, Dizzy Gillespie, Krupa, Duke
          Pa tah pa pa tah pa pa tah pa pa tah pa
          Brmm brmm brmm brmm

Feeling it through the old wood of the floors,
That long vibration as if the cosmos
Was all made up of stretched skin and guitars.
      Woody, and Big Bill Broonzy, Miles and Philly Jo,
      Bonham and Freddy Mercury, mountain music and blues,
Sidemen half-gone in the old vinyl,
Guys in Saturday bars a long time forgotten,
A long and good time ago.

And no, I'm not ready. No. Nor alone.
Still dreaming those long green farmhouse dreams
With however many or few,
On this excellent planet rocking out
The good old cosmic blues.

Just, now I know, when the time comes, as times do,
There's excellent music right next door,
There's damned fine drumming in the other room.

2017

BARNEY'S HOUSE

Dream takes me to the house of our old friends,
As if we're coming off the road, after a long trip.
The house we walk into smells just as it should:
Old redwood, red wine, that wonderful
Korean beef dish she used to make.

(Reality says, our old friend
Doesn't live in this sort of place anymore.
Reality says, his wife,
Whom I loved, and clashed with, and loved,
Is recently dead.)

But dream sweeps us on from room to room,
Spotting here known lovely things, and other things
Lovely and new.

In this room, some small grand-daughtery girls
Spin in their tutus,
Reaching skinny little-girl legs
For elegant shapes
As an older girl directs them.

Next door, a pack of little boys crawling fast
On hands and knees,
Romp by like puppies.

Now suddenly a great dark lawn,
Sky overhead. Stars.
Small clumps of people sit on the grass
In the near-dark. Glasses clink. Little sparks
Of matches or lighters
Flare in the dark, light up faces.

The amused bark of laughter
Rises from intellectual argument,
Along with names rising like bubbles.
Schopenhauer. Marx. Freud. Jung.

And the next room is bright with sunlight
Through just-installed windows.
Plasterers are finishing walls in here,
Laughing as they work.

On a sawhorse, a portable radio plays 50's jazz.
The workers are wide-beamed, big-bellied, gray-whiskered, naked
As the day they were born.
They wave and smile and keep on working.

And here's our friend, in the very last room,
Which is unfinished, sky blue beyond the beams.
Smell of new-cut wood.
Hands in his back jean pockets, he surveys
What is to be done.

"Barney," I say in this dream,
"How many rooms will the place have
When you finish, about forty?"

He grins. He looks about forty.
"Yeah, maybe," he says. "When we finish."

2017

About the Author

Edith Rylander was born in California in 1935, grew up in western Nevada and coastal California, and moved to central Minnesota in 1964, where she has lived since. She and her husband and writing partner John D. Rylander raised three children (Daniel, Shireen, and Eric) while living as closely and kindly to the land as they could. They raised livestock and vegetables, harvested firewood and maple syrup, built two houses, including the earth-sheltered home where they currently live, and for many years raised most of their own food.

She began writing poetry at age eight. Her first literary publication was in a Bantam Book called *New Campus Writing #2*, in 1957. Her work has appeared since, sometimes at long intervals, in numerous literary magazines and a number of anthologies, and in the collections *Dancing Back the Cranes, Hive Dancer, Dance With The Darker Sister,* and *Wrestling with the Angel,* the latter three collections all with Red Dragonfly Press. She has also been the recipient of two Bush Artist Fellowships ('80 and '91) and a Loft-McKnight Award (1994).

Edith has also collaborated with her husband John on a memoir, *Journeying Earthward,* and a teaching text for poetry, *What's in a Poem.* For more than thirty years she was a columnist for the St. Cloud Times, Morrison County Record, and Long Prairie Leader. Some of her journalism has been collected in *Rural Routes: Essays on Living in Rural Minnesota.*

All of these years and interests are reflected in the poems of *They've Packed up the Rock and Roll.*